Empath Healing.

The Survival Guide for Empaths and Highly Sensitive People using Emotional Intelligence, Cognitive Behavioral Therapy, Psychic Empath and Vagus Nerve To Become a Healer of Yourself.

[Dr. Stanley Leary]

Legal & Disclaimer

The information contained in this book and its contents is not designed to replace or take the place of any form of medical or professional advice; and is not meant to replace the need for independent medical, financial, legal or other professional advice or services, as may be required. The content and information in this book has been provided for educational and entertainment purposes only.

The content and information contained in this book has been compiled from sources deemed reliable, and it is accurate to the best of the Author's knowledge, information and belief. However, the Author cannot guarantee its accuracy and validity and cannot be held liable for any errors and/or omissions. Further, changes are periodically made to this book as and when needed. Where appropriate and/or necessary, you must consult a professional (including but not limited to your doctor, attorney, financial advisor or such other professional advisor) before using any of the suggested remedies, techniques, or information in this book.

Upon using the contents and information contained in this book, you agree to hold harmless the Author from and against any damages, costs, and expenses, including any legal fees potentially resulting from the application of any of the information provided by this book. This disclaimer applies to any loss, damages or injury caused by the use and application, whether directly or indirectly, of any advice or information presented, whether for breach of contract, tort, negligence, personal injury, criminal intent, or under any other cause of action.

You agree to accept all risks of using the information presented inside this book.

You agree that by continuing to read this book, where appropriate and/or necessary, you shall consult a professional (including but not limited to your doctor, attorney, or financial advisor or such other advisor as needed) before using any of the suggested remedies, techniques, or information in this book.

Table of Contents

Introduction

Ever since I was growing, I loved to give people all of my attention when they talked to me because I wanted to understand everything bit of what they said. I also wanted to reflect on what was unsaid and connect the dots. I notice that a lot of times, people would tell me things and stop halfway, probably because they were not sure they should tell me more for one reason or another. Other times, I would sit and stare straight into the speaker's eyes, listening and struggling to read meaning to what they had not said. Trying to see if I could understand their silence, feel what they feel and read what was on their mind.

In fact, I was bent on discovering more than the spoken words of my friends that I often paid attention to everything each person says and everything they don't. Their gestures, postures, silence, tone and so on, I read them all. But hard as I tried, it was a failed experiment. I could only say a few things about them. Fine, "I can tell what they would likely say when you ask them something, I can tell if they would like something or not, and that was all. why should you do this, you know he hates it!" I still could not tell how exactly they feel about something.

I can't tell what is going on anyone's mind too, no matter the closeness. The human mind is simply too hard to read and you will likely be hoodwinked, no matter how you try. Some persons are pretty good at hiding their emotions too, they will hide what they feel or think so perfectly that it would be too hard to guess. You can't try too hard if you still appreciate your sanity.

Along this line of guesses and quest however, I discovered something interesting. Some people actually have the exact talent I was dying for. These people are humans birthed with a supernatural ability to read the mind of other people. They know exactly what you are thinking and they can spell out the words in your head. They can tell you how you feel and they can point out the exact spirit that is driving you as you speak with them. All they need is to engage you in a long talk and at some point, they would begin to tell the next things you were going to say. The shocking thing is that they might even share your feelings and dump whatever they felt initially.

That is really weird, isn't it? And that is exactly why many people think it was some supernatural power. I just used that word too. But in reality, that word and anything like it do not qualify these people. They don't have any special or fanciful powers like those eastern witches you see in pre-medieval movies. They are just humans, purely talented ones, and Empaths is the name coined for them.

There is a lot of surprising things about Empaths, and you will wonder how they manage to do those things. How do they hack into someone's soul, understand how the person feels and even share feelings with that person? If you are just bitten by an Australian snake and you feel that horrible pain, trust me, an empath would feel the same thing if one is around. How does that happen? I promise you are about to find out in the next few pages. Just make sure you miss nothing.

Empathy has different grades and types, and the most awkward news about empaths is that many don't actually know they are one. Frankly, you could be an empath and you wouldn't even know. I do not know for sure whether you have got the blood of one running in your veins or not, but I can assure you, you will understand what exactly an empath looks like by the time you are done with this book. You will learn detailed information about how to spot an empath when you meet one, and the various ways an empath can exist. That way, you can tell whether you are an empath or not.

I guess you are beginning to wonder if I am an empath too, and you'd better get that idea out of your head right now. Nature didn't organize a selection test for us, it just went on and selected some random persons, minus me. So, I gave up trying to be one, but I appreciate each one. They are doing exactly what I have always wanted to do, the level of care and concern they showed to others can change the world if we have enough of them. And that is why I have spent years and grants researching them.

Did I tell you that empaths have problems too? Well, they have problems in some ways, and their love life, work as well as relationships always have complications than other casual people. In fact, growing up wasn't a piece of cake for most of them, as you will soon find out in the eye-opener dangling between your hands right now.

If you are an empath who desires to learn the full stretch of your power, how you can navigate life and resolve your immediate problems using some well researched and proven styles, you will find important tips and direction in this book. If you are just a curious person with a fanciful interest in empaths too, I am proud to tell you this book contains practically all you'd like to read.

I have to warn you at the same time, there is quite a lot to be unlearned. The main reason you are reading about Empaths is that you have heard about them somewhere and something seems irresistibly crazy about them. That is fine, but we might have problems at some point. Why? Because my guess is that up to half of what you heard about empaths isn't right. There are so many fallacies trolling the street that it is hard to tell facts from fiction.

This is why you need to drop off whatever you have learned and see a different perspective. I guarantee you are about to discover the planet of empaths and how things run in there. Get your favorite drink, be sure it is an evening on the couch and open the next page, time to empath-travel.

Chapter 1: What Is An Empath

An average dictionary reads that an empath is someone who thinks they understand another person's feelings. But is that all? I bet you know better. The world of empath is a strange and uncommon one, a complex one that cannot be captured in 2 pages of a dictionary. Some people know no more than the description in a dictionary, and that is why you would find confusing articles here and there. You would need to take your mind off everything else you have read before you read this, it is the best advice I could give to anyone who truly wants to understand empaths.

To start with; how much can you say about the feeling of other people around you? A lot? Little? Nothing about how others feel? Try to remember how you relate with your new friends, old friends and those you care about, it will bring your emotion to light. You will be able to tell whether you cared a little, a lot or you were very concerned about what they felt. This reminds me of a young client who walked into my office on a late Friday. 'I am too heartless and I want to change!' he cried into my ears. He was fuming in anger and frustration, but I calmly showed him a seat and listened to his story.

He was a man who didn't give a hoot about others' feelings. He would break up with his girlfriend at leisure. He would pick her call and hear her rant in madness. 'how the hell could you do that? how dare you mess with me?' He would hear the helpless lady change the tone of her voice to promise him heaven and earth, to ask him to return to her and forgive her for things she didn't do. Despite that, he would remain unmoved, no matter what anyone had to say. It was the same in all situations that people appealed to his feelings. Even when he decided to grant their requests, it was not because he was moved, rather he was pressured or he hated the intense pleas. His heart was a sort of hard rock that you cannot change by pouring soft or harsh words on it.

I have seen soldiers cry for their beloved. I have read about an assassin who found his target and had the perfect opportunity to pull the trigger but couldn't bring himself to do it. The radiant smile of his unsuspecting target got to his heart. He became overwhelmed by emotion, picked his gun, walked away and confessed his crimes to the world. These sort of things happen everywhere, that is why sometimes, you want to punish someone for hurting or disobeying you, and you would change your mind after their remorsefulness touch your heart.

But the other side exists too, some people cannot just bring themselves to care for others. Even when they try. These people suffer from apathy, narcissism or psychopathy. What are those?

We will talk about them some lines later, but first, what is empathy and how do these things relate? Empathy is a state of the mind that your mind connects with the mind of others in kindness. It happens when you can see in people's glasses, I mean, you can see through them by looking through their eyes. You stare and listen, and you would understand what exactly they were seeing; fear, excitement, worry, hope, and so on, whether they say it or not. You can see things the way people see them and you understand where exactly they are coming from.

To use the words of Sigmund Freud, 'empathy is about putting oneself in another person's position'. Empathy is psychological, it is purely about the state of the mind of two people. Two persons of which one has the psychological balance to read the other person's mind with compassion, he can understand and share the feelings of the first person. He can also tell how the person may react or what the person would do next. An empath has the ability to feel empathy; compassion, not just for humans, but also for life, earth, water, everything you can imagine. He can imagine what you are passing through as you speak with him, he can feel your pains the exact way you are feeling your pain and he can correctly imagine what you are thinking about.

Some years ago, I heard the story of a young schoolteacher who met a truck driver. This truck driver had just lost his dad and his children in an auto crash. As if that wasn't enough, his wife filed for divorce a short while after and he lost his job because he couldn't concentrate on the wheels anymore. After losing his job, he would sit at the stairway of a large cathedral and sob quietly, paying attention to no one and getting no attention in return. One day, this schoolteacher came around and saw the truck driver in tears. She began to console the driver and she persuaded him to share what he had gone through with her, he did. And guess what? She shared his pains. She broke into tears and began to cry with him. She left him after a while and cried home alone. She was never the same person. She lost interest in her job and quitted too. 'Life is harsh' she scribbled on her walls, 'life is deliberately wicked to many' she wrote further. She stayed indoors most of the time and planted some Aloe Vera in a few pots in her room. After a few weeks, she was found in the room, dangling by a rope in the ceiling.

Many people cannot imagine why anyone would kill themselves over the pains of another person. Even the cops thought there was more to it. They searched for more clues and conducted series of investigations. In the end, they found her suicide note and realized that she had murdered herself. The series of poems she wrote also explained that she had killed herself over the pangs of sadness that she felt when she heard the story of how a man had everything and lost it all. Nobody knew this man she wrote about, the nearest cathedrals were checked and no man was ever found on the hallways. Could he have killed himself too? You already know as much as I do about him.

The schoolteacher never assumed she was an empath. The word was not found anywhere in her books, walls or writings. This means, many people may be empaths and they would have no idea. One thing was sure at least, she forgot how she felt before she met the old man. Everybody who knew her was sure she had little trouble with life, but how could she get so emotional that she would wallow in the sadness of another person? Empathy.

Empathy is the only emotional state that works that way. If you imagine yourself in the shoes of the schoolteacher, do you think you can feel the man's pains that much? Many of us can feel the pains of other people, we can even feel so sad that we would cry for their loss but certainly, we are not losing our sleep over it. I have to say I belong to that group. You might lose sleep in your own case, and possibly be moody about it in a few days. But all that could still be out of deep sympathy, or probably, you have some traits of an empath or you are still developing your strengths as a full empath.

Now let me explain the different types of emotion I promised, though you must remember, I have only selected the most relevant to what we are talking about.

Various Types of Emotion

a. **Sympathy**; Sympathy is what it means to feel bad about what has happened to other people. For example, your best friend has just lost her mom. Your wife got fired. Some strangers got burnt or injured in a fire disaster, and such sardonic cases. It is okay to take a deep breath and feel sober for a while. You see this sad news on the TV, listen as a friend talks about them or sit beside victims and hear the stories. You would feel depressed as a person who feels gloom, 'I am so sorry' you would find yourself saying to them, out of pity. That is exactly what sympathy means, the show of pity. Sympathy is an emotion an average person should have. Though, at different levels. I have friends who would tap your shoulders and tell you 'I am sorry man', then walk out on you. They are not being harsh or insensitive, it is just their level of sympathy.

Some would stay a while longer, 'I really wish this is not happening to you, you are clearly a nice guy that everybody loves and you don't deserve this beast of a disaster, they would say. But in the end, they needed to move too. You don't expect them to lose their sleep over your worries.

Let's consider another practical situation. You lost a contract and took to drinking, you locked yourself in the house all day and emptied the bottles. It didn't matter how hard or dangerous the drinks were, you only wanted to keep drinking, as long as it helps you avoid thinking about your loss. Your friends came around, listened to what happened, made you understand that it's not worth it, and went back to their homes. Of course, you got better while they spoke, but it didn't go away like a flash.

Deep in the night, you were still wide-eyed, thinking about the cars you could have bought if you got that deal, the party you would have thrown and the smile of victory you've been hoping to play on your lips. You still feel bad about those things, and you are up at night over it. Your friends feel sorry too, but what are they doing? Snoring! Does that mean they don't feel bad? Certainly not, that's just how sympathy works. I feel bad for you, but it really is you and your problem. Sympathy can lead to empathy, but before we discuss empathy, take a look at this:

b. **Apathy**: it is not always the case that a person feels sympathy, a lot of times, some people feel nothing to whatever happens. They are purely indifferent, neither

11

excited nor sad, just neutral. They have no reservation or resentment; it is just a lack of feeling they cannot help. An apathetic person doesn't feel excited about his job, the squash game or the lacrosse player. Whether you are happy or not is out of his business because he is not happy himself.

Sometimes, anger and some of your past experiences may make you or your friends take up an apathetic attitude to life. Those times are when you walked in from school and announced, 'mom! I got the role in the drama'. She wouldn't even look at you, and she would give you an "okay" with a smile with the corner of her lips. That was not what you expected right? Well, she wasn't sad about your success, but she felt nothing special about it. she may have felt it last year and rushed you into her arms, but this time, she had just lost her job and nothing else seemed to matter.

A lot of times, apathy is the reason a man would ring his wife from work to tell her that he's just got his promotion. What does he expect? She ought to jump and pierce the third floor with her screams of excitement. But what would he get? 'oh, congratulations' she would manage to say and find a way to terminate the call. Such behavior is expected when the wife had just lost something precious to her; her dad, mom, friend or gold bangles. She would feel complete indifference to whatever you feel, without a way to get herself out.

This is one of the things I want you to understand. Sometimes, your friend could be in a mood too neutral to share your joy or sadness, and you must not hold them on it. They have their own emotion to battle and this is probably one of those times they are actively battling it. Find a way to cheer them up. Remind them of something they adored, play tricks on them, surprise them and force them to retract from the new mystery they are drowning in. That is when they could return to share your joy.

More often than not, apathy is a damning behavior with dire consequences. You can never feel bored or excited if you have an apathetic mindset. You don't care whether you have just lost your wife or car, whether Australia is on fire or your little kids may die if you don't get the job. You are just carefree about everything. Remember my client I mentioned earlier? He was just like that. He didn't even care about the tears of someone he had told he loved. But apathy is not inborn, it is a result of some sad experience, and it can be overturned with mind-blogging experiences brought about by friends, beloved and counselors.

c. **Psychopathy**; A psychopath is among the wildest persons walking the earth. Their beliefs are odd and their style is not enviable. With similar ideas to an apathetic mind, a psychopath also cares little about what happens to any other person on earth. Usually, they are not concerned about themselves or anyone, they simply live, grow and die. The only notable difference is that while apathetic people do not care about anything, a psychopath cares a lot about pleasure. They enjoy fun, they merry when they desire, but they don't give a hoot whether you think what they were doing was fine or not.

Most times, they deliberately do everything the society hated. They take up the sort of behaviors you last wanted to see in a gentleman or lady, just to prove that they are defiant and they don't care what happens. They enjoin everything the State is at loggerheads with; illicit businesses, drugs, and a sexual urge that cannot be satisfied easily. They don't care whether you like them or not, whether you think what they are doing is right or wrong, they just go on and their 'thing'. Even at those times a doctor tells them they are dying, they think it is all bullshit and continue pipping whatever the doctor says was killing them. Death means nothing anyway.

d. **Narcissism**: It will help you a lot if you know about narcissism too. They are passionate people who lived like psychopaths. They cared little about others and you really cannot do much to convince them. But they shouldn't be mistaken for psychopaths, there are marked differences. While apathetic people and psychopaths would not care about what you think of them, narcissists are different. They want to know what you are thinking of them, in fact, they want you to tell them what they are doing is the best too. They are highly emotional and all their emotion is for themselves.

They can read the mind of other people like an empath, but rather than get immersed in the feelings of others, they would look for ways to manipulate the thoughts of other people to suit their own interests. Whatever anyone says that doesn't support them will be thrown out like a heap of rubbish. It is always a very bad idea to have someone like this in a position of authority. They form dictatorial governments and lead with no mercy. They keep finding ways to make themselves happier, richer and wealthier at the expense of their subjects, and anyone who thinks they are wrong is seen as an enemy. Nobody is always right you know, sometimes, you should let things slide and allow people to have their say even when you think you are right, that is one thing you can't ever get from a narcissist.

e. **Empathy**: The most complex of all: empathy is the greatest humanitarian feeling a man can nurse. It is a situation when you do not only feel sympathetic to a person's cause, you can also feel what they feel directly. Their pain is your pain, their sadness, joy, and success is your success too. It is more popular among lovers. When you see your lover smiling, you would naturally smile back without even knowing why your partner had been smiling. You would gladly persuade them to share their thoughts and you would begin to feel exactly what they feel as you listen to them. It happens between sisters, allies, parents and children and close relationships. If your partner loses her contract and refuses to sleep, you would most likely stay up too, trying to get her to let things go, even though you feel just as bad.

For natural empaths, they do not even need to hold a very close relationship with you before they could hack into your spirit, understand what you feel and show you compassion. They can go farther to hold such relationships with animals, plants, earth and other things you cannot imagine. A series of medical researchers have tried to show how this may happen.

"Their 'mirror neuron' is hyperactive," says Hans Fenwick. The mirror neuron is a neuron in the brain that facilitates communication with other people's thoughts and ideas. It makes it easy to mirror the inner brain and mind of others. You know, like a mirror that helps you see things you wouldn't have seen. An empath may also transmit other people's thoughts to themselves through the electromagnetic reaction between their brain and their heart, especially when listening to those people.

From the discoveries of Tricia Burke, there is a chance that having an excess of dopamine which is a neuro-transmitter may also trigger empathy. Besides the chances of synesthesia. What is that? your brain's ability to pair things together. It is why listening to some music can relive some memories. Staring at a picture, a movie or even a dress can bring some scenes in your head et cetera. That feature is super sharp in an empath's brain, another reason they can easily link the words, the sight that goes into their brain with what more or less, what runs in your head.

According to the famous Dr. Judith of West Carolina, it is also possible to directly feel what other people feel through emotional contagion. This is why other

14

members of your staff may panic about the office after you have just slammed one. It is the same reason every child in a hospital would burst into cries the instant they hear the cry of one.

They are empathetic from birth in most cases, and they tend to understand everybody easily. They are usually quiet and attentive, paying attention to details nobody cared about and surprising everyone by telling them things they didn't know about themselves.

They usually grow to be spiritual, and that is why they can feel the energy of the spirits around when they close their eyes and lay quietly. Probably, they can see those spirits too. If you are an empath, you will be liked and naturally respected by everyone. People would like to share your pains and happiness with you because you always seem to understand. We all have that friend that looks so dumb to us because he is never angry at anything. He is always quiet and he gets along really well with everyone. He also hates watching the news or listening to horror tales of the number of victims. At every opportunity, he avoids coming in contact with violence.

Empaths worry about others much more than they worry about themselves and that is why they break into tears quite easily. You might say they are boring, but you should know they are as boring as the person sitting beside them. If you sit beside an empath and you are happy, he is likely happy too, if you have some negative energy like anxiety, fear and so on, let one sit beside you and he would soon pluck those from you.

Most people find it hard to be their friends because they don't want to stay with a person who seems to see everything like a mirror. They don't want to be an intimate friend anyway. It isn't that they don't want to have a friend, but something in their spirit prefers the company of animals, plants and someone who deeply understands them too. A reason they would rather stay in a beautiful garden and stare at the lakes than jump about a party room with a cup of drink in their hand.

I am starting to wonder at this point; does one of these sounds like you?

Chapter 2: History Of Empaths

You might be wondering; How did empathy even begin? Who were the first empaths, how did they live and how did their genes survive to date? How well were they accepted? Was life always the same with them? Empaths seem like caring being, how did they manage to survive and still exist in this heartless world? Those are good questions. We need to find answers to them for us to grasp the full picture of what empaths have always been. They were questions I used to think about too, and years of research have finally brought us the answers.

First, empathy is a form of human feeling, just like happiness, sadness, fear, and sympathy. That means it has been around as far as humans have been on earth themselves. 25,000, 15,000, 6,000 years ago? Nobody can tell for sure, but we certainly agree that humans have been around for quite a while.

The effort of historians and related fields has proven that the people of the past have developed a lot of things that are similar to what we have today. They have probably made those things according to the resources they had, their customs, their needs and so on. They made everything across the various spheres we now have today; Engineering, Psychology, Medicine, Arts and virtually all fields of research. This is why each of these fields can trace their origin to the distant past.

To cite some examples, I will remind you that most drugs are made in the laboratory today, but it is scientifically proven that natural drugs, natural foods, and unprocessed products work better. We also know that some herbs and plants can bring a smile to our faces if we eat them more often. They can cure, prevent infections and so on. You remember any doctor saying that? That is exactly what the old men believed too. They researched and found many helpful plants. They discovered what you could cure or prevent those plants and how you should do it. Though, I don't think they know about the microbial infections that are rocking our world.

In engineering and technology, you have heard about the pyramid in Egypt, the Crystal Skulls that nobody knew how they were made. To mention just a tip of the whole mystery. Empathy is a field of research too, though not as broad as philosophy, history, and others. It has attracted interest from various fields and scholars who keep trying to explain it in detail. Historians, Psychologists,

Sociologists, Primatologists, and Neuroscientists are among those leading the game.

Despite the fact that there are no strong references, we believe that at some point, empathy must have surfaced in the history of these earlier inhabitants of the earth. The famous story of a father who went wild because his son was struck is my first pointer. In that story, the boy was struck in his chest by a poisonous arrow from an invading army that attacked their clan. The father cried in harsh pains and became heartbroken as he watched his only son writhe in pains. After a while, the father lay flat on the mat, right beside his son and slammed his eyes shuts.

In a way nobody could explain, he began to draw the venom and pains of the poisonous arrow from his child to himself. He was sweating intensely as he did it, and soon enough, he began to bleed from his heart. Everyone became silent as they saw what was happening, sobbing quietly. He began to sing the songs of pains and horror. He rendered poems on suffering and sacrifice and he went on till he drifted into unconsciousness. At that same time, his child who had become unconsciousness began to move, and gradually, he gained consciousness. That was empathy from a very old story.

From what we believe, a lover must have watched someone she loved groan in pain. She would shed tears as she watched him complain of one thing or the other. Soon enough, she could feel the pains herself and she could feel them forever if he eventually died. She would feel hurt, remain sad and unhappy for the rest of her life. She would wish she had died for him, died with him or at the least, share some of his pains with him.

A lot of famous stories report that while a lover was in Town A, his lover in Town B can sense that something was not right somewhere. Perhaps, she would be up and doing, having fun with her friends and joking about the weather when she would suddenly feel an impulse. She would realize something was not right and jump on her feet, agitated. But where and how something is wrong might be hard for her to tell. In the end, you would learn that something devastating had happened to her lover in the other town, just about the time she became suspicious and agitated. This tale was common among the wives of brave warriors who left their homes for war. That is empathy too.

The story of witches is another popular case. You probably don't know that it is a common custom to arrest, detain and prosecute witches in prehistoric times. That custom was still maintained until the 14th century in England. Usually, anyone found guilty would be seized and hanged. That may not sound bad, but the problem was that there were no clear methods to detect a witch. Once someone raised an alarm that you are a witch and you got arrested, there was just a little chance that you will not be prosecuted. That way, many people were unjustifiably detained, prosecuted and murdered.

A lot of empaths were often victims of this problem. They felt other people's pains and they could sense doom from the air in the atmosphere. They could add up the facts they gathered from a person's situation and easily tell the next step a person would take or what else might happen to the person. This is why kings at the court, and to date, policemen usually invite empaths to help trail a criminal or suggest what could be the next step in an investigation.

In fact, if they met you for the first time and you managed to tell them a bit about yourself, they could tell you the rest about yourself. They tend to know more about a person than he knows about himself. They often avoid a large gathering of people too, preferring to stay among animals or plants.

Out of brilliance, they were often right about what they say and people thought they had some strange powers. People hated that what they said often came to pass and feared they could do more than simple predictions, perhaps they could cause harm to other people or cast spells on them. So, they labeled them witches. They were often arrested, tried and hanged, and that was how most of the empaths in prehistoric times were wasted. Many decided to shut their mouths and hide whatever they feel, but they end up giving themselves away and falling into the usual pit of death.

The story wasn't better in the days of the Spartan community. They were very strong people who loved nothing better than war. They gave all forms of warfare training to their children from a young age, and they often capture a lot of slaves.

A few times, they gave birth to physically weak children who could not withstand all the military training from early life, and what happens? They kill such children themselves. It is the same thing when they give birth to children who seem to be weak emotionally. Such children would cry when asked to supervise a group of slaves working on a farm. They would burst their lungs and cry out in horror as they watch the helpless slaves laboring to get their jobs done. The older Spartans considered it a big weakness, and they made it a law that any child who felt the emotion of servants and showed it would be hit with a death club.

Despite these historical problems, empaths are still alive, walking everywhere on earth like other people. You might be wondering how they managed to survive all along. They were hated from the past, often killed and criminalized, but we still have them on earth. You should try not to be surprised. They will surely exist like other human beings forever. This is not because empaths can be made with softening your heart and training, it is something bigger. You may train yourself to become an empath if you really desire to be one. But the real gist is that empaths are not made in most cases, they are born as empaths.

They do not decide to be empath themselves. They just grow to find themselves deeply concerned about other people. They spend all of their time and energy on other people and sharing the physical, mental as well as the emotional pains and struggles of the people around them. If you have an empath around or you are one yourself, you will notice their excessive love for other people. It is not clear whether each of the many communities in the past gave a name to empaths. But we call them "empaths" today of course.

In history, we know many were called witches in Europe, China, and America. But that is not even a peculiar name for empaths. Some other people who were not empaths were also called witches. In particular, women whose children or husbands often die. Of course, those women didn't kill their loved ones, the deaths were due to health complications such as blood type, chronic infections, blood infections and so on. They were usually innocent of the crime they were accused of, but they were executed anyway. Empaths often shared the pain of people like that too, and they often had no way to help.

Whether any community in past times realize that some people are born with the ability to read the mind of others was a tough question. Nobody can answer for sure. But if they realize, they must have given them a name which remains mysterious too. But if they hadn't then, that fact wasn't known to anyone until the 18th century. In fact, the word 'empathy' was coined by Edward Titchener around then, and it was coined from the German word *Einfuhlung*.

The earliest research into the nature of Empaths began with Germans (Willhiem Wundt, Rudolf Harman, Fredrich Theodor, and so on). It gets broader with Englishmen, Americans, Swiss and a few Italians. In the words of Carl Jung, one of the first few psychologists to provide full reports on the topic, "Emotions are contagious. We now understand from our years of research that it is absolutely possible to unconsciously mimic another person's emotion to the point of feeling exactly what they feel".

Subsequently, neuroscientists have made a revealing discovery. There is a neuron known as the 'mirror neuron'. This neuron makes it possible to see and imagine things going in the brain and mind of another person. Every human has it, but it works better in some of us than the others. You remember I told you about it in the last chapter.

In case you don't know that you have it, it is what makes it possible for you to look at everyone around right from when you were 7 months and above. Then, you begin to study and try hard to mirror their language. You see someone smiling at you and you stare at them really hard, trying to understand what they were communicating. Later, you understand what they were doing and you would shine your toothless mouth back at anyone who smiled at you. Your mirror neuron helps you imitate how people walk too, and it is exactly why a baby would cry when it thinks everyone around it is crying. Are you connecting the dots? I bet you are.

Study the children around you. You will notice that as they grow older, some of them relate better with their parents. They walk virtually everywhere with them. When their parents are angry, they try to get angry too, and when they see their parents smiling or asking them to smile, they do it. That is the root of empathy. If this behavior continues to their adulthood, they will become helplessly submerged in other people's feelings and they can do nothing about it.

For some others, their mirror neurons didn't grow to be that active because they do not share their family's feelings to adulthood. They probably grew rebellious or as it often happens, the family didn't grow happy enough to keep such behavior up.

These types of people will feel sympathy at different levels, not empathy, and for the odd class (apathy, psychopathy et al); their mirror neuron hardly developed beyond infancy. They imitated other people as they grew, but it was always for survival. They were raised in a terrifying environment where death and danger were always around. Everyone, including their parents or guardian, was extremely harsh at them and they were always scared. They felt that survival was naturally difficult and it shaped their minds.

Did I reveal something about the kind of child you might be breeding? You need to think about that, let's continue.

Chapter 3: General Types of An Empath

If you ask me, there are different ways you can be an empath. We will call them the types of empathy, and there is a lot of them. Some people think it is just 3, some say 5, 11 and so on. The list is endless. It depends on who you ask and how much your source knows. There are a thousand and ten ways to describe anything, Empaths inclusive. But there are certain ways that seem common and accepted among modern-day experts and explorers. Remember I warned that you need to forgo a lot of the things you have learned because most are not exactly right. That is why you should not feel surprised to see that some types of empath are listed here and you have never come across them. You will surely find some you have read somewhere too.

To begin with, I am glad to inform you; I am going to clarify the tales you have heard too. That tale that an empath must hear animals, feel the sound of plants, do this and that and so many things that made you unsure whether you are an empath or not. Some even assume that if you cannot perform all the skills of an empath, you are not one. That is not right, since, it is possible that you are an empath with more than five talents, or just a few. You only have to check the following types and see where you belong. If you don't belong to any of these types, you probably aren't an empath yet, you may need to let nature take its course.

Now, to make sure you don't miss anything, I will classify the types of empaths into two. They are not contradictory; they are just different ways of seeing the same problem. Here we go!

Types of Empaths
1

a. **Cognitive Empathy**: cognitive empathy is about your ability to think. Not just think, calculate. Look at a person and imagine what they are thinking. Try to understand what each of their gestures is saying about them. If you are a sound cognitive empath, you can easily stare at a person giving a talk and decide if the person was being honest or not. You can scent arrogance, pride, honesty from whatever anyone says by merely staring at them. Narcissists are really good at this, and it is a reason some scholars are still insisting that narcissists are some sort of Empaths too.

A lot of times, it is very hard to read a person's thought because they can deliberately hide all the features that could make people read their mind, they would say something and perfectly pretend as if it was their true belief, but of course, it wasn't. You would not understand people like this by staring at them, you need to spend more time listening and trying to understand rather than trying to find out if it is true or false. That is one way to boost your cognitive empathy. Try with your friends first, then strangers.

b. **Emotional Empathy**: this is the next most important. Actually, many people think it is the only type that exists, but as you see, it is just one on the list. So, what is it about? It refers to the ability to feel other people's emotions. While cognitive empathy focuses on the ability to penetrate, see, and share the thoughts of a person, emotional empathy is all about feeling what the person feels.

For example, Christie, an empath explained to us in an interview that she attended the convocation ceremony of her kids at school. "While on a seat, I watched a student come up the podium, he was going to render a talk on 'friendship', he had memorized the talk so he had no trouble reciting it. But he thought the exact opposite of what he says. He had no friends and he hated friendship, but because he was selected, he came on board and spoke about how valuable friends are. I can tell what he thinks by listening and studying him intently, I could share his thoughts as a cognitive empath"

If I was an emotional empath, it would be easier to read his feelings. I can tell if he was anxious, happy, worried, confident or uninterested without speaking a word to him.

c. **Compassionate Empaths**: Americans like to call them the Heyoke Native American Empaths because they seem to know it all. It is the most complicated of the three types of empaths discussed in this section. They feel or think what their target is experiencing, and they make sure they do something about it.

If you notice that the boy who came up the podium was not confident, you would walk up to him and encourage him once he steps down. That's the specialty of compassionate empaths; they include action. In another case, you would know what your friend was thinking after he had just lost his job as a cognitive empath, you would know how he felt and share his feelings as an emotional empath and as a compassionate empath, can you remember seeing people's problem and at the same time digging hands and legs into it?

It is okay to have one, and the three can work together in you. Some other people can feel these things as they sympathize with their friends, but as an empath, I can tell what my friend thinks more accurately, and I can provide the best solutions.

Types of Empaths
2

a. **Claircognizant Empaths**: My guess; someone has mentioned this in your ears before. It is a very popular type of Empath. It refers to people who have a special ability; to know. If you are a claircognizant empath, you can tell when something is not right. You may suddenly jump out of your chair in a law court and scream at a witness giving account: 'you are a liar!'. Of course, every eye in the court would turn at you, and the judge would be tempted to ask you how you got to know, if she wasn't furious enough to send you on a jail vacation.

Well, if the judge faced you and asked 'and how did you know he was lying?' you might still bag a vacation to a prison. You have just disrupted a court proceeding, but you were right! You knew the truth, but how? You can't tell. Apart from lies, you can tell who is right, what is right, or what is not and who is not. You can tell when someone is hiding something or isn't being real too. It's a great gift, but one that can you land you in jails for having no proof. Just the same way it was fatal for people in old times.

b. **Physically Receptive Empaths**: Another name for empaths like this is Psychic Intuition Empath. An average physically receptive empath is a dreamer. If I was one, I would stand in front of you and dream about your physical features. I would dream about your strength, weakness, heights, pains and so on.

It is a skill that combines cognitive, emotional and compassionate empathy. It sounds simple and straightforward, doesn't it? Right, it is. if you are an empath who has this power, you'd have to use it every time you desire to heal someone of their immediate pains. What you need to do is penetrate the spirit of your target and possess their physical features. Do you remember the man I told you about? The great empath who died and saved his son from a poisonous arrow. It works similarly, empaths share the pains of whoever they are trying to heal, and in the process of healing their target, they dry up their own energy as the target gets better. They will be fine after a short while. Empaths who have this skill aren't so common in town these days.

c. **Flora Empaths**: some empaths have a special ability to deal with plants. They understand the energy of plants and they know how much each of the plants can do. If you hear that a suspected empath enjoys staying in a garden alone, you shouldn't be surprised. She is probably a flora empath and she is making attempts to understand the power of that plant. Flora Empaths are quite common. It is also possible that every empath has a bit of this power, though they seem to appreciate plants more than one another.

If you are a full flora empath, you will have the ability to listen to the whirls of the trees and make meanings from it. You can tell the plants that bring good luck and success from those one should never touch. When your cousin gets some flower and decides to place it somewhere in the room 'hey, get that out!' you would shout, because your instincts report that there is something bad about the plant. In another case, 'hey, give that to me' you would persuade him and keep that flower somewhere special in the house. A special altar that the plant spirit asks you to keep it by penetrating your own instincts.

Now you see that as an empath, you do not only penetrate and share the human spirit, you understand plants and animals.

d. **Fauna Empaths**: Talk of empaths who understand animals, and there is a fauna empath. These kinds of empaths were the most popular in prehistoric times, and that was why people assumed they had some extra-terrestrial power. What is their specialty? They understand animals as much as you understand human beings. They can read the mind of an animal, they can listen to an animal and tell what exactly an animal is scheming.

In most cases, a fauna empath can tell whether an animal, especially a pet is being possessed by some spirits or not. Not only do they hear the animals and understand what they are saying, but they can also interact with all animals.

The most astonishing thing about fauna power is that it is the most undiscovered power today. Sometimes, some animals would stare at you and communicate. Without making a sound, you think you can hear what they were trying to say too, but you would discard it while trying to focus on you'd get them out of your hair or how beautiful it looked. You didn't notice that what you thought you heard was part of reality.

Notice yourself, if you are beginning to control the dog in the house silently. If you notice that without speaking a word, you can control a cat or tell it what you are thinking and it seems to respond, then I am most likely talking about you. You have a skill you can develop by putting it into use every time.

e. **Medium Empaths**: The Medium Empath is the spiritual empath. He can listen to the spirits when they walk into the house. He can see spirits patrolling the kitchen or sitting where Dad was about to sit. Medium Empaths usually have a tough life. Nobody takes them seriously and people prefer to think they are going insane.

If you have that power, you probably have the world in your hands. Spirits understand everything that happens on planet earth, and they can help you every time you need it as long as you are in good relations with them. You have to note though, being a medium empath comes with its problems. You may sit in the living room when a spirit walks in. It sits directly opposite you, looking straight at you and telling you what happened in the other world. Your unsuspecting mother might come into the living room at this time and desire to sit in the exact spot your spirit visitor was sitting. You would try your best to warn her. 'no mom! There is someone in that chair, use the other end or get the next one!' when she looked around and find no one, she would stare at you curiously, wondering what the heck you were talking about. Then she would begin to think you are losing it and everybody else would think that way.

f. **The Telepathic Empaths**: Telepathic empaths are the traditional empaths. The easiest type of empath that comes to anyone's mind when you mention empaths. They are the type who can sit in front of you, and listen while looking into your eyes and telling you precisely what you are thinking. They can take note of your gestures, your unspoken words and your reactions to accurately determine what you are thinking.

They are the type I called cognitive empath a short while ago. In modern days, they do not even have to sit around you. They can read your books, your autobiography and a true piece of information written about you. With that little piece, talented telepathic empaths can think of and tell the next step you are planning to take. This is why modern police like to invite telepathic empaths when investigating tough criminal cases. Once this kind of empath read up the facts available on a criminal, she can shut their eyes and go into unconsciousness. Trying all their best to connect with the mind and thought of the said criminal. More often than not, they are successful.

g. **The Geomantic Empaths**: Any empath with geomantic capability can interpret the signs of the earth. They seem to have listening ears for nature and natural occurrences. All they need to do is see and listen, they would accurately read the signal each natural circumstance was bringing or predicting. Intense sun tomorrow? Nice cozy weather ahead? A rain ditching day? Is the wind giving a fair warning? They can hear and interpret it too.

If the world had enough of them, we probably should not consider astrology. They know it already. They can foretell whether an earthquake, inferno or some natural disaster of any sort is about happening. But many reasons could complicate the existence of geomantic empaths.

In the first place, a lot of them do not even know they have the geomantic empath talent, and this means they will never feel up to the task. 'why would I do that?' each one would ask themselves. At some other times, some would causally notice they have the talent, but it would look like a joke to them 'hey! Bet your bottle, the sky will be blue all through tomorrow, no sun!' they would bet and as you would expect, win. But that's all they do with it. Rather than bet away their talent, they could employ it in a bigger, more productive use. But they don't even know there is a talent.

h. **Psychometric Empaths**: Psychometric Empaths are sound physicists. Who knows, the founding fathers of physics and psychometric were empaths. That was a joke. But psychometric empaths are sound individuals who can see nothing in something. They can sense information from pieces of non-living objects and they can feel the spirit in such objects too.

Don't be surprised when your kid suddenly rushes into your room, claiming that the teddy in the room stares him, or the water jar is threatening to punish him. Kids can be unpredictable, but they have the tendency to see and feel these things more than an adult. If your child runs to you every time to report one object in the living room or the giant statue in the hallway, your child is probably a psychometric empath. He can see them and he can listen to them, and he is threatened because he is too young to build self-confidence, the only entity that would make him walk among them all without fear.

Once you notice that you can read non-living objects, you can tell when a spoon is about to break, an electronic is about to develop problems or your trouser is planning to tear, you have a skill that you really should hone.

i. **Intelligent Empaths**: Intelligent Empaths are found in the academic system. They are a bunch of people who cannot explain how they do it, but they are far intelligent beyond their age. They don't spend such a long period of reading, and they remember everything they scanned with their eyes, much more than those who read it with all attention. They outperform every other person in their field too.

Is that beginning to sound like you? don't get too excited. There is another part you need to examine. Intelligence Empaths can read jargon. When they come across some words they have certainly not seen anywhere, they can read and provide accurate answers to such words. Does it still seem I am talking about you? Here, you have my hat if it is a yes. If you got a 'no', please, return my hat.

j. **Precognitive Empaths**: Precognitive is the most common type of empaths that everyone usually regard as 'any other person'. Though, they are renowned for their predictive ability. They are not seers or soothsayers, and nobody thinks their instincts are especially powerful. Their instincts may suddenly arouse a spirit in them, giving them a sign that something is about to happen. You remember I once mentioned a lover who lived in Town B while her husband was in town A. She was at ease with the other people until she suddenly felt an impulse. She knew something was going to happen, but where, when and what were not questions she could answer. A person who has such skills is most definitely, a precognitive empath.

In popular reports, precognitive empaths know what is about to happen. They know where and when too, but they usually have no power to stop the occurrence. For example, a child who dreamt that his father left for work and was shot on the way. Such a child understands what exactly was about to happen, but there is hardly a dad in the world who would take the dreams of a little child serious. 'It is just a dream sweetie' His father would tell his with a hug, and he would drive out to die in the raining bullets of street mafias. Sometimes, an empath like this would become overexcited for no valid reasons. She may suddenly become anxious, agitated, restless or her heartbeat would double its pace. Sometimes, one would suddenly get curious and frown her face. Whatever comes to their mind was where the problem was.

For instance, if your emotion suddenly changes and thoughts of your best friend filled your head, call him immediately. Tell him whatever you can think of and make sure you keep him in touch.

From the past few pages, I have shown you that an empath has a lot of powers, and you are probably one. It is not necessary to be one, but if you are reading this book, you have definitely seen some signs and you are eager to find out more. Now, you know more, and you can judge whether you or one of your friends is one or not.

Chapter 4: How To Know If You Are An Empath

Have you read my last few chapters? Then you would be getting the hint already. There are clear signs that you will spot in anyone or yourself if you are an empath. There is a lot of them too, and I have made references to some while talking to you in the past few pages. But I have to spell every one of them out for emphasis and clarity.

Remember I said it, I am about to tell you 20 different signs. If you found just one or up to six, you are most likely not an empath. You are only emotional, maybe highly sympathetic. But if you find more, say seven to fifteen, there is no gainsaying that fact, you are among the living and talented empaths that can save the world; have fun while hunting for yourself:

a. **You are the odd guy**: the easiest sign of being an empath is that you are the odd guy. You are the only one who does the weirdest everywhere. At home, at school, at work, everywhere. You are just the girl who wouldn't do what every other person is doing. Friends are hanging out tonight, not you. Everyone was talking about the movie they saw and that famous artiste, it's none of your business. Everyone thinks the parliament is driving the country crazy; whatever. You might want to check the next list, you are possibly the guy I am talking about.

b. **You hate the public**: That's just like the first thing we talked about there. It is not about being an introvert, extrovert or any kind of vert, you hate the public and there is no two-way to say it. At the slightest opportunity, you are out of the dining, and straight to your silent, self-run corner in the room. Right, when the bell rings, you are out of the public gleaning eyes and nosy talks at the office, down the street and straight to your house, no dinners, no hangouts, no extra talk with anyone, you just want to be home. If that is you, you are my prospective empath.

c. **You are in the know about strange things**: In some awkward way you don't know yourself, you always know when something is not right. You can stare at a person giving a speech and shake your head, 'something isn't right about this'. Most, if not all the time, it turns out you are right. You are the only guy who wouldn't smile when mom returned with a brand new car. Why? what's wrong with you? Everyone would ask, but you don't know yourself, and you want to tell her to get that car back to the seller. But it doesn't make any sense and you don't find the words to tell anyone. You dare to tell your sister and she thinks you are crazy, you don't have a choice, you give up. A few weeks later, mom crashed in that car. You have always had the instinct when something is not right. Isn't it? Does that sound like you?

d. **You can read a heart like a book**: This is the craziest part of your skill. You can stand in front of someone and see right through their head. You know exactly what they are thinking and it looks like you can read their thoughts. You are a natural lie detector. You just give that sly smile and play along when someone tells you lies. You didn't see them or catch them red-handed, but you strongly believe it is all a fallacy. Though you were always attentive and you have never pulled the show off for them. In the end, you realize they were wrong and your instinct was right again. When someone isn't saying the whole truth, you only need to pay attention to their words and thoughts and you could rip the truth from them.

e. **You are the emotional hacker**: This is something you try to mask every time. You realize that your heart breaks easily and you don't want anyone to think you are soft. But the instant you listen to a dying old woman telling you her stories, or the helpless little boy telling you about his family, you would break into helpless tears of emotion. Feeling the exact pains those people are going through and wishing you could lift them out that second. It is the exact thing that happens when you watch movies. You can feel the pains of the actors and you find yourself crying in front of the TV. Actually, that is why you would rather walk out when everyone else sits on the TV. It is a strong indicator that you are an empath, especially if you forget everything else about you and you became overwhelmed by the feelings of the person you have just heard.

f. **You are everyone's go-to**: despite the fact that you try to avoid everyone at every chance you get. You remain everyone's go-to. Everyone thinks you are nice, calm and you have listening ears, so they would always be at your door. They have come to tell you what their boyfriend did, what happened at work and why they were on suspension. They have come to listen to your advice. They want your motivation and they believe that you are just the girl who understands and never sees anything bad in them. Even strangers who would just use your table in your restaurant, or ride beside you on a larger bus. If this indication gets stronger with you, you are probably an empath because people would come to you only because you can read their mind and you understand, then you have the right words and spirit to heal them. That really sounds like an empath.

31

g. **You are extremely passionate about humans**: why would any leader be corrupt? Why shouldn't every leader lay their life down for their followers? You can't ever find the answers to those questions because leadership is a big deal to you. You would rather die than not put the interest of your followers at heart if given a chance. You hated the thought of hurting your followers and you scheme about how leadership should be all-inclusive and every right should be respected. Of course, you always feel awkward and unsure about participating in elections, voting, campaigning or contesting, you dream it nonetheless. Am I talking about you?

h. **You can pick illness like a flash**: You know, doctors and most medical experts think transmission of diseases is usually due to some factors that nobody can tell for sure. That's not a problem. But a reappearing fact is that people like empaths have the power to share or transfer illness too.

If you have that sort of power, you would visit a friend one day, find her in a sickbed and shut your eyes right beside her, will all of her visible illness to yourself and equally share that sickness. That's something most people would never want to do even if they have the power but empaths love to do it. In the twinkle of an eye, their skin would begin to steam, the sickness transfer is happening.

Your case may not exactly be like that, but if you notice that you have the power to control the physical illness of people (especially cases like cold, catarrh, body pains, and eye infections) and share some of them to yourself, you might need to up your skills, but you are the empath we are talking about.

i. **Lower Back and Digestive Issues**: Are you aware that there is a part of the human body that stores emotion? It is called solar plexus chakra and you'll find it in the center of your abdomen. You will begin to feel some inexplicable pains from that part the moment you are about to take on the emotion of another person. Once in a while, you would feel hit on this spot by something heavy and harsh, and you would go down on your knees, clutching your stomach in your hands. It doesn't happen all the time, but you will be able to tell when it happens; what you feel is your stomach is beyond what Doctors could hope to heal. You may have complained to a doctor, but they would find nothing wrong with you, alternately, you are left with only have suggestions which don't change you a bit. For an empath who can imitate and feel the emotion of others, the stomach disorder, and lower back ache are complementary features.

j. **You have an eye for the losers**: now this is something that could sound a lot like you. As an empath, you would turn the TV channel to a boxing game and pay full attention. you feel every hit in your head and you dodge with every wave of the boxer's blows. Of course, you are dodging and hitting yours in your sit. But the notable part is that you would feel pity. You would feel sorry for the loser. You do not feel he should win or not, you are only concerned about him. Rather than share the victorious sheers of the winner, you are the type who would think about the ego, the pains and the humiliation of the loser. You would do it even if you were a big fan of the winner. Boxing is an example, you'll do the same thing when election results were announced, when a football game was played and so on. This sounds very much like me actually, you need to see me watching basketball. But it isn't enough to call myself an empath.

k. **You are always on the run**: how come I am just mentioning this? It doesn't matter anyway. The point remains that you are always on the run from everything. It is something to have a phobia for the crowd, it is another to always want to start again. you have that too. you would always wish you could close your eyes and every pain would go away. You wish you would not listen to the pains and pangs of people anymore. You try to get drunk and irresponsible just to drown the sorrows of other people that keep ringing in your head. But nothing ever seemed to work. You would still listen tomorrow. You would still share pains and offer help without thinking twice tomorrow. There's no doubt about this too, if this is you, you are an empath.

l. **Tiredness**: For reasons you cannot explain, you could feel drown out easily too. You do not feel the vibe and rigor that every other person feels and you are just your quiet, tired self. You would feel weak after taking on the physical or emotional features of other people and the disheartening part is that nothing can cure you. Drugs, sleep, comedy skits, nothing cures you and that goes on every day.

m. **Creativity**: Yes, that is the word. Because you are often quiet and trying hard to provide solutions to everything, you turn to be creative. In solving problems at home and at work, everyone likes to listen to what you have to say, they are always dazzled by your way of solving problems. That is not all, you can compose beautiful songs and it is usually about life. about friends, people, and nature. You are pretty good at writing and you have for singing and drawing. Most empaths do not like to act.

n. **You want your world**: you are not always excited by the prospect of living a great life in affluence and controlling people. You don't feel triggered when someone talks about living a large life of expensive cars and fanciful houses. All you want is your own world. You want to walk in your garden quietly, alone. You want to stare at the goldfishes for hours and smile at the blooming summer. You enjoy being in your own room, by yourself, doing whatever you find convenient. Even without leaving your own room, you are sure you have enough to do all day and night.

o. **You are a domestic plant yourself:** As an empath, you likely share this fanciful fantasy for plants that you could pass off for one. You are always in the garden, staring at them and listening to their silent waves in the cool weather. When driven by your energy, you can begin to imagine the plants speaking to you too. It often seems like you hear each word passed and you can understand. You can feel the energy of a flower, you can hear its angelic calls and you know where it would be happier in the house. You strongly believe that the plants can hear you, so you spend time talking to them as you walk by each of them, and you think they can talk back. This is a hard skill. Because if you truly do not hear those plants, it could be a sign of some mental or psychological illness. If you hear it, people will still assume you are going crazy anyway.

p. **You are a pet freak**; This is next to the earlier feature. You will love animals a lot if you are an empath. The special love empaths feel for animals drives many to become vegans. And they would rather be hit than let you hit a crazy cat on the road. An empath would carry their pets everywhere and every time. And with time, they can hear what it thinks and what it is saying. You can hear not just your pet if you are an empath, every other animal. Psychologists and Modern-day Neuroscientists have problems with this feature. They are struggling very hard to understand if it is possible to hear these animals or it is an improper malfunction of the brain that makes it seem like reality. There is no discord just yet, but if you can feel, along with other supernatural talents, you simply can.

q. **You listen like it is everything**: Another peculiar talent of empaths is that they listen like it is the best they could do. They would remain quiet and attentive as each person shows up and share all their life problems. They would neither argue nor debate. Once in a while, they have helpful suggestions and they are always willing to sacrifice their time. As you would guess, this talent comes with some other skills and it requires a lot of endurance and patience. Empaths have those in bulk.

r. **You can sense the day**: Once a few times, empaths have the ability to read the day. If you are the type who would wake in the morning and look around after yawning 'Oh! This is going to be a beautiful day', and your predictions about the days were right, you are probably one of the empaths. Empaths can feel the day and its energy, they know when the day seems dull and unhappy and could bring bad luck, they know a brilliant day even when the sky looks gloomy. If you have ever sat beside anyone who looked around and declared to you 'the day isn't giving a good sign', you should never argue with them about it, even when they had no idea they are empaths, they might be.

s. **You hate second-hand stuff**; Empaths are people who feel self-confidence and would fight to maintain it. They lose their confidence and get irritated when made to use second-hand products. They feel uncomfortable and they can feel the feel spirit of whoever used the dress, shoes or car in it. Even when it looks all immaculate, they would never feel happy in it. If this is how you feel in a second-hand product too, it could be another sign that you are one of those I am writing about.

t. **You are your own plug**; Lastly, empaths are their own source of motivation. They are all they need to ever get started again. They have shared a lot of spirits. They have heard a lot of pains and tears and fears, they are battered by the mixture of experiences in their head and conveniently, yet, they can motivate themselves. Empaths often result to addiction to get out of their problems. They would sometimes drink to drown their worries. But this should not happen in your case. You can remind yourself that you need to be available to help others, and that's why you must never get tired or weak. You must become a lawyer so you can agitate for the helpless people whose voices drum in your ears, among other intrinsic motivations. Empaths are always self-motivated, are you?

Phew! I have listed all twenty as promised. Now go through them again and give a deep reflection, are you or your best friend one?

Chapter 5: Thriving As An Empath-Protect Your Energy

Ask any empath, they don't know how, but they hardly have the energy to do anything. Always tired, worn-out, and looking for every opportunity to jump into a bed, and immediately pass out. If you observe yourself well enough, you will realize you are often dizzy, quiet, and weightless. You cannot muster the energy to do anything serious most of the time, yet, people will never stop coming to you.

Being an empath is no reason to become a living and lifeless sadist. You should be alive, agile and happy. You might feel that way once in a while, but it would hardly last the passing moment. Your radiance would fade out after you discuss with just a few people. You need to protect your positive energy, you need to thrive above the negative energy that radiates people and their problems, and you need to stand out as the power light. This is the only way you can help people out of their problems.

This negative energy that makes you weak, lifeless and unhappy is a result of the negativity you have absorbed from other people, and the emotional vampires who have sucked your positive energy out of you and replaced that with negative energy. You may not get that energy from them, but the following are surefire ways protect you, and can help you thrive as a lively empath with a positively driven energy;

a. **Know when to draw the lines**: Drawing the lines is necessary for all empaths. You must know when to stop listening and protect your energy. Sympathetic people who can do it without blinking an eye; remember I mentioned some of my friends who will simply path you on your shoulders and walk away. As an empath however, you might find that hard.

When you visit your friend and she begins to cry about her husband who has remained unconscious in the hospital for some time, you would also get emotional. You would forget you were drained at work and you would offer to put the kids the bed for her. Or perhaps, stay by her husband's bed. These things can further sap the life out of you, and you must know that when you should not do them.

As a talented person, your instinct tells you when what you are about to do will cost you a lot of time and energy. You must listen to your instinct if you want to protect your energy. In fact, negative energy radiates from some people. You may be positive and alive before you meet them, but the atmosphere would change the moment you sit beside them and listen to their problems. Have you noticed anyone like that? Stay away from them, after all, it is much easier to protect your energy by preventing the negative energy from radiating to you. Also, there are other people who will share their problems and your soul would not become weary. You would share their pains but you would remain optimistic enough to heal them with your words and spirit, without damage to your spirit. So, when it is clearly not fine by you, say no and try to be firm!

b. **Have a backup system**: Your soul is a very special one, but you must maintain it the way you maintain other people's souls too. Other people come around and you share their mental, physical and emotional experiences, you share their worries and make life look simpler for them. You need a way to get the same thing for yourself too. So, you might want to answer this question; what do you enjoy doing at leisure? What is that activity that can lift your spirits and raise your positive energy? Aren't there people who want to listen to you too?

Take all the time you need and think about it. You will have to fall back on those activities every time you need some good vibes. Is jogging your thing, how about dancing? Eating is what works for some empaths. I can also assure you from my years of research and experience, most empaths enjoy writing and singing in the walls of their room. Whenever they feel bored, tired, and weak, all they need is to sit on their favorite chair and begin to write. Without having anything in mind earlier, they often write about what is making their heart restless. They put down their wishes and what they would do if they have the chance to go back in time. They would compose songs without much thought, and before you know it, the negative vibe is lost in the outpour and they are sizzling with a good feeling.

Besides that, you can look forward to your parents and immediate friends or relatives. If you are in a hostel where it's not just you in the room, your roommate needs to know too. They need to understand your nature and how it can make you feel lonely and weak. Don't make them guess and don't assume they know, summon up courage and talk to them about it. It is true that many often stigmatize empaths but it is no reason you shouldn't try. They are the nearest to you and they will likely understand that this isn't your doing, anyone would get out of an empath skin if they had a choice. But you are in it, and they are all you have.

c. **Dwell in the power of water**: Water is the most powerful natural resource on planet earth. It can heal you in ways you did not think about. This is why I often suggest that even when an empath listen to people, they should hold a glass and drink as they listen. If you are able to drink consistently throughout the conversation, you will certainly maintain your positive energy even after you have unconsciously hacked into the speaker's spirit and you can feel what they feel.

For example, a colleague who invited you to dinner to disclose some personal issues was talking to you. She was considering quitting her job and running away because her boss was harassing her sexually, but she was afraid that she might never get a job after the records say she left her former job without a solid reason. If you can consistently drink water as you listen, you would feel pity as if you were in her shoes, but the negativity in her emotion would never radiate to your positive energy. The result is that your positive energy would thrive and you can easily advise her or do more listening.

The power of water does not end in drinking. Ruthann's research in 2015 has proven to everybody that naturally and supernaturally, pouring water on your body can cure your spirit. Let the water stream down every area of your body. Sometimes when you deliberately shut your eyes in the bath, you can almost feel the tingling spirit of excitement running through your veins. No matter how tired you are or how negative your felt, getting a good bath in water can boost your spirit. You can immerse yourself in water for as long as people. You may shut your eyes and envision yourself jumping up and down a beautiful lake or waterfall in the early morning sun. Some experts recommend using a spa bath or a bath in the rain too.

d. **Self-Discipline**: I know this should be the first, but talking about it now isn't such a bad idea. You need to control yourself in order to save your energy. You have a form of energy that the world needs every time, you will surely feel that urge to jump into a problem and offer some help too.

But you can't do it every time. You should start by taking note of how you spend your days. Are you always trying energy sapping activities? How about those you relate with, are they the type who are always draining your energy with their negativism? Think about it, is it the Dick and Harry that would always want you to think life has been wicked to them only? You need to check who you spend your time with. Did you even make out time for your own pleasure? Create a better environment for yourself. A positive energy does not come to an empath from what they eat, it is from what they feel in the environment.

e. **Create a quick control**: If you are in a conversation with a convicted woman for example, she is in the jail and she would be hanged pretty soon. Though it was all for nothing she did wrong. Her husband and his brother had died of food poisoning in her house, and she truly had no idea how that happened.

As an empath, you'd definitely feel her pains, you understood what she was trying to say that the court would not listen because she had no proofs. You are the seer who can look into her eyeballs and believe that she is telling the truth, but you cannot do anything to prove her innocence. You will definitely feel hurt too, and you might begin to shed tears of sadness which would drown your positivism. It will be too hard to even drink water in a situation like that, this is why you need a quick control.

You may teach yourself a phrase and let it ring in your head every time you need to control yourself. Make it something like 'I am strong and I must remain positive for humanity'. 'I am powerful and I will provide solutions to this problem', you can also change that to any line that might work for you.

That aside, notice your respiration. Your respiration is likely to change when you are feeling very sorry about something, perhaps, you would start breathing at a faster pace because your pulse has doubled its rate, it could also be that you are now breathing at a slower pace, ending your breaths with sigh. Either of them is bad, you can get a lot better if you manage to return your breathing to your usual relaxed pace.

Lastly, you can ground you worries. What is that? You ground your worries by connecting with the earth and shedding all of your problems into it. If done properly, the earth will absolve all of your doubts, negative energy and replenish your soul with a vibrant living energy that can keep you going again. How should you do it? Get yourself into a very quiet environment and lay flat on the floor. Turn your eyes up to the sky and rest all your body joints on the ground. Shut your eyes and begin to think positively. Tell yourself about your strength and positivity, shut your eyes and let loose in unconsciousness. By the time you find your consciousness, you are the whole hero again.

f. **Carrying healing stones**: Carrying healing stones can ensure that negative energy does not gore your spirit. You can keep one in your left palm every time you go out. Experienced empaths believe that positivism can radiate from these stones every time, so it is nice to have one around. They can always cleanse you of every negativity lurking in your spirit too. Considering their skills, I recommend you make this one of your quick get-away method.

What stones can you consider? I am about to mention 3 different stones that can do the magic;

i. Citrine: Citrine is the stone called eternal sunshine. Any of those names can help you find it in a store. If you look beyond how beautiful it looks, its ability to radiate positivity is a reason you should keep one around you. It spiritually radiates positivity that can permeate into your spirit and keep your vibrant energy alive, especially if you are a geomantic empath. It can also influence the circumstances you are handling and make the best to happen.

As a practical instance, if you have enough citrine in your bag while speaking with someone who fails his exams every time, they would begin to tell you why they think they failed and together, you can positively find out ways to resolve the problem. That would happen even if the person used to be negative, perhaps if not for the citrine that was influencing his environment, he could have kept lamenting in rage 'my lecturers are crazy!', 'my parents are the problem'. Rather than face his own failures. He would also find faults in every suggestion you make. This is why stones like that can make your service a whole lot easier.

i. Calcite: Calcite is my second best. It is a beautiful stone that you can find in many colors. And be rest assured, every one of those varieties can do exactly what you want. They can boost your spirit every time, they can invite good luck, prosperity and happiness, they can also fight off negativity. Some native wiccans in the United States believe that empaths should get as much of this in their home every time. I guess not having this was why the schoolteacher killed herself. Do you remember the schoolteacher who hanged herself out of pity for a man she met at a catholic church? I trust you didn't forget that story.

f. Tourmaline: tourmaline is another important stone you may try out. It is used for all sorts of protection, especially if you can find black tourmaline. It can protect your physical and spiritual self and it can also cleanse your spirit. Good enough, it can be found everywhere and it isn't usually expensive.

g. Technology: Now this is interesting for a lot of reasons. Do you know you can help your energy through the modern technology? It is something a lot of people do not know and it is one you will surely enjoy doing. All you need is your mobile. There are energy oriented applications on the internet that you may download. Golden Proportion, Virtual Oxygen, Cleansing apps and so on are among those that can you give the boost.

Now that you know how to thrive as an empath and protect your energy, do you think you can ever be sapped of life or negative thoughts could get to you? For the first time, cheers, your answer is mine.

Chapter 6: Empaths And Relation To Love And Sex

Being in a relationship with an empath is like waking to a pot of gold beside your bed. From the records and interviews, I see that they are much more valuable in fact. But relationship is a big thing for empaths, something larger than any other person would like to see it. Empaths have a completely different way of viewing things in a love affair, their definition of love, sex and relationship are entirely insane to a random person. This is one reason it is sometimes hard for them to maintain a scintillating love life, and being in a relationship with one can seem like a death mission, instead of an adventure.

How do empaths view things in love and sex? Those are two different things, and I will talk about them one before the other. For empaths who grew old without finding a true balance in their love and sex life, I am about to show you where you got it wrong. If you have had no love life and sexual experiences in your own case, I am about to reveal a love map that can give you the direction to tread all through your love life.

Also, if you have had a few already, but you need more direction, you need to pay complete attention to the next few lines. This is the easiest way you can make sure you are not going to spend the rest of the years jumping in and out of people's hearts and allowing anyone to drag you into fruitless relationships. Ready to talk about it? Sex first.

Empaths and Sex Life

Empaths usually belief that sex goes beyond getting out of your clothes and getting into the skin of the other person. They see it as getting into the life, the soul, the spirit and alliance with the other person. This is why as an empath, you would find many people sexually attractive, but 'heck!' your mind cannot bring you to get down with them. Because you have no real contact with their soul. You don't just want their body, you want to have sex with someone who shared feelings, thoughts, and seem like a partner for you. I won't be surprised if you got drunk, had sex with a random person and the next night, you begin to find that person about the bar.

Perhaps, you might build that connection. You hate temporary things, even when it is sex.

An empath does not enjoy sex when it is with a random person, even though it isn't entirely prohibited. That is why they would hardly agree to a one-night thing, and if they did, it is purely out of their burning craze to fulfill their sexual call. They really want to look in your eyes as you ride on each other and see love flow through your eyes to their heart. They want to feel what you are feeling, hear what you do, share your energy and connect with your soul.

It would be a frustrating fun for them if they could not read a thing about you while you are into each other. And 74% percent of empaths who responded in an interview believe that they prefer a silent sex. The type where both partners do not utter a word with their mouth, rather their heart. If they ever say anything to you at a moment like that, it is either they are drunk and they have no idea what was dropping from their mouth or they want you to feel and believe every single word of it. You can hold them to anything they say at a moment like that, they mean most things they say anyway.

So, if you are not an empath and you're considering having random sex with one of them, I have to wish you a strong luck because it is a dead end you may never escape. They would want to connect with you again. Also, if you are an empath fantasizing an amorous night with a complete stranger, I am here to say that it is not going to end that way. Your instincts will be there to tell you it isn't right again, and if you refuse, you might be falling prey to another heartbreak. So, am I saying you must have sex with only one partner with whom you exchange love?

No, that is not it, I am only saying there must be a mutual relationship between you two-way before you begin sex. Also, you are also safer from a poor sexual life if you choose a partner, your love partner as your sex partner, because sex has something to do with love to you.

I'd love to end this by telling you one fact, sometimes, it is possible to find someone who returns your love and still have a tough time getting in bed with them, it is not abnormal. Your body is probably just finding independence. Your body would naturally treat everyone the same way while you are less mature, that is one other reason you suffer heartbreaks for everyone. You feel the twinges even when it wasn't all your affair. But as you develop and become established, you will be able to create a separate love for some other people. You will be able to value them according to the sensitive seat they hold in your life and you can easily gel with them. One of them is your lover-sexual partner. You can speed up your sexual life recovery by taking tantra sessions with an expert.

Empaths and Love

This is a very broad topic, I should probably be writing a complete guide on it, though the coming lines will explain all you need to know. So, how do empaths treat love? There is just one word for it- heavenly. Empaths see their love life as something they would die if they dare walk away from, and that is one reason you can be sure an empath will never cheat you in a relationship.

Here are the key features of an ideal love life of an empath;

a. Empaths often give it all: If your dream is to date or get married to someone who would give it all, an empath is likely your answer. Empaths are mostly ladies and they would rather die than cheat. They are the type who sacrifice their job, time, money and all that they have just to see a smile on the face on someone they love. They would do anything to keep you two bounded, and strong above all temptation. I am trying to think it is my imagination, but I believe they are the direct descendant of that 'Ruth' in the bible who left all she had and followed her in-law out of love.

b. They are open to a fault: Honesty is a code to empaths. You know better if you are an empath or you have had a love affair with one. They would spend all of their life making sure that they don't play games with their love. That is why your empath-girlfriend or boyfriend will return home and tell you about how they had been invited by their boss to a date, and how they had turned down some for you, or accepted some for business reasons. You need not worry about them, just sit back and show them love, they aren't going anywhere.

c. They expect a complete commitment: As much as empaths give out all the love they could muster; they expect the same. This is why you should try to give back the love you have enjoyed from them. Show your partner how much you appreciate their love and you are trying to match their sacrifice, and they will stick to you. You can't possibly meet the love an empath gives if you are

45

not an empath, and if you are an empath, it is good for you to understand your partner can only try, they don't know half what you do about love. You will easily let go of their inadequacies if you let that sink in.

d. The communication is all about their partner: This seems one sided sort of, but it remains a fact. An empath is head over heels in love with you, and they would do more for you than any other person. Remember that they are born listeners and solution providers, and they will try to listen to your problems and find infallible solutions. Your success is their success, and they want to see you do it. If you are in a love affair with an empath, don't be surprised that they will hardly talk about themselves, you are the subject at every meeting.

e. They love too much too: As usual, this ought not to be the last, but is probably not a big deal as such. Empaths are highly emotional people who fall in love with body and soul. Once they are in love with you, it is hook, line and sinker. Nobody is taking you away from them and they are not ready to step an inch away from you. Sounds ideal for love, doesn't it?

Unfortunately, it isn't all rosy like the summer garden, empaths have always had a lot of complications in their relationship. Those complications usually result in constant heartbreaks and instability too. You need to tackle them with your partner before they bloom into real issues. They are;

a. They sense too much: It is no news that empaths are hypersensitive beings. They read meaning to everything. They can spot the tiniest change in your behavior. They know when everything is fine and when you are beginning to find a PLAN B to their love. If you draw back in how much love you used to show, they can feel it immediately, even if they decide not to show you. Some of these feelings are actually unnecessary, they can be overlooked because the partner ends up returning to the way they were, but it could become a sore in the heart of empaths.

b. You can't hide any personal feeling: I remember telling you that the mind of an average person is as open as a book to an empath, how much more can we say about their lover? You are like a transparent mirror to them. You have no weakness, no plans, no strength that they don't know about, and that is something most people don't like. 'How could I be like a transparent paper in your eyes?' 'For goodness sake, can't I have a thought of my own?'. It is a relationship, but many hate it when even their weakness seem to be in the open.

c. They are moody: This is something a lot of partners find hard to cope with. Empaths are prone to emotional attacks and mood swings. You may get moody without a valid reason and not even your partner will understand because you do not understand yourself. How then can you explain? It is worse when your partner is in a really good mood, they keep wishing they could get you happy and the atmosphere remains hard to understand.

d. They may begin to ask for space: Even when there was something irrelevant as a blip in the relationship, empaths may begin to ask for space. Everything might seem perfect a short while earlier, and then they show up to tell you that you need to get going or they need to take a break away for a while. 'What is the problem honey?' you would try to ask, but the answer would never come. Gradually, that relationship turns to a mess. 'I am not going to let you drive me crazy!' you will hear their partner slam as they walk out on our empath. You are not going to let that happen in your relationship, are you?

e. Lone soldiers who assume too much: Empaths assume too much. They think you already know; they think you are doing this because you are trying to pay them back for what they did wrong. They assume you are just being deliberately wicked. They keep playing mind games when you the other partner is in complete darkness about it. If you are an empath, you would assume your class teacher can guess why you didn't do your assignment, your boss most likely understands that because you looked sick at work yesterday, you won't be showing up at work. Because you told your partner you are not fine by the shoes he bought for you, he would understand why you threw them in the baggage. You may be right. But tell him, don't assume, and don't let him guess!

f. They don't express their needs: Empaths are not used to relying on people for their needs. They are so used to this form of life that it is often hard to open your heart and begin to share your problems. They listen to their partner's and others', but they solve all their own problems in their heads. They only present solutions. A lot of love partners hate this, because it practically means such partners are not intelligent enough to participate in their career, besides, it is no partnership.

g. They still go far with other people: If you are an empath who got married to a non-empath, you shouldn't be surprised that they will find it extremely hard to tolerate your openness, except if it is clearly supported by them. A lot of lovers do not understand why their lover had to spend all of their time listening to the private life and innermost part of some other people. They believe that their empath-partner should discuss personal issues with them alone, but the caring nature of empaths will make this impossible. It raises distrust and insecurity feelings in anyone who loves an empath, another tough problem.

h. They love you but they can do without you: This is something a lot of lovers hate to hear too. Empaths love you to the moon and back, but they can live fine without you. They have suffered enough heartbreaks to get extremely out of hand if you decide to leave them someday. Everybody hates to be told they can leave, but that is just the way empaths are.

So, my dear empath, can you see where you got it wrong? Have you seen the part you need to pay more attention if you are going to make anything out of that relationship? Let's discuss something else.

Chapter 7: Empaths And Work

It is important to understand the work life of an empath as much as you understand their love life. That is precisely why the work life of an empath is the next big thing on our table. Why should you know? Because this is how you get solutions to all uncertainties you feel about your work. Your mood swing, your insecurity feeling, your friendlessness and so on. I am going to talk about why they may happen and how you may get yourself out of them.

Above everything else to be mentioned, remember we all do different jobs and we meet different demands, and as a result, some of the things may apply more to you while some others don't. I'd also like to inform you that to make sure you understand perfectly; I will be splitting this into two. First, the usual experiences you may have at work as an empath, and I will attach how you may tackle each that sounds like a problem. After all, you can't just quit every job because you face some problems. Thereafter, we will see about the jobs or professions that suit you best as an empath and those you should steer clear of. All ready? Let's move.

Empaths at work.

Like the bright sun in summer, empaths are very easy to spot at work. From the way your new staff thinks, talks, sits and look around, you can instantly tell if you have just hired an empath. For one recurring reason, they are always different. Look for these features if you guess you have just employed an empath, and expect these things to happen if you are an empath yourself:

a. **They are never comfortable in the opening**: if you are the type who hates having to sit among tens or hundreds or people, you are likely the person we are talking about. You will find out that it is not a big deal to talk in the public, you can do it but you simply hate it. You'd rather walk into the office of your boss, get a seat and sort things out with him. You will certainly stick to the last seat at every opportunity, and you will try to avoid being held by what you said. If your office is in the open, perhaps a noisy place or an open unit where you have to listen to the deafening noise or you attend to the counter-quiet crowd, you will hate every bit of it. Once in a while, it is a great idea not to restrain yourself from giving your opinions in the public.

b. **They overwork**: As an empath, you will observe whether you hate your job or not, you would always work like a robot at your jobs. You would rather spend extra time at the job than leave it undone. You hate being at the center of distraction and you would always avoid any inadequacy that would make the boss stride in and begin to slam you. Everybody seems to hate it too, but empaths are extra careful with their job, and you would notice that if you have just one or a few empaths in the office.

c. **They hardly network**: A lot of people will hang around after they are done with the day's job. They are waiting for their friends. You should notice them sitting in 3s and 4s. They are dining and banting about various issues. They spend what some like to call unpaid overtime, and they don't mind how long they do it. But if you check the circles well enough. An empath isn't among those people. Your empathic staff was already off the instant it was time, otherwise, he stayed behind and was busy completing some urgent tasks. You should have noticed this from high school if you are an empath. You hate to be around a second after the clock strikes.

d. **You don't like the job**: this is the confusing part of empaths. They don't always enjoy what they do, but nonetheless, they do it. You could grunt about it to your employer or your few friends, you often do the best of your ability when you can. But you are on the lookout too, always patient and hopeful that one of these days, you would grow to like the job or the job will get better. As an empath, you should learn not to grow too weary of your job, especially if you have got no other just yet.

e. **Loyal to the tip**: one set of people you can trust in your company are empaths. You don't need to keep an eye on them, all you need is to identify the empaths at work and make them understand that you trust them, then wait for impressive stats. You won't even wait for recognition as an empath, but if it comes, it becomes the huge boost you need to drive yourself crazy at work. You would keep working hard even when everyone else thinks you are going crazy or you are driven by a greedy desire. Also, you would become uncomfortable when people discuss rumors and after-work tales about your employers, partners and organization. Loyalty is your talent, use it every time.

f. **You fight mood swing:** One big problem you are tackling at work is mood swing. You are all dressed, confident and flamboyant before you left your home earlier in the day. You might even maintain that smiling face and exciting spirit to work. A short while after, you don't know how but you have lost that spirit. You do not feel half as excited as you felt when you came in, and all you wanted was to head back into your corner soonest. If this happens every now and then, it is a prove that you are an empath. Empaths hate long hours and they really don't survive it. Your best bet is to cut the hours short or get out of that job.

Empaths and suitable Professions

Why do you even need to 'get out of a job' if it was all perfect? A job that seems inconvenient to the point that you'd jump at anything else is not your original fit. You may look qualified for it on the papers, and it may even seem the only thing you have been trained to do all your life, but if it doesn't work for your nature as an empath, the fact you should embrace is that it is not your fit.

Letting that ring in your head can make life very easy for you. You won't struggle in occupations that will drain out your energy. You will feel confident to walk out of that job that makes you unhappy and yes, you will know exactly where to earn a living without hurting your nature.

To help you do those, I am going to begin this part by listing the common areas you shouldn't try working at all as an empath. If you are engaged in any of them already, then you are directly having a firsthand experience of the features I listed a few lines earlier. And what to do? Best is to quit. The unfit jobs? Here:

a. **Police:** Being a Police officer can be challenging for an empath. You can't cope with the trauma of unrepentant criminals and their soul keep penetrating into your souls. You would love to see things from their own perspective rather than get straight at your job and bring culprits to justice. You will never enjoy the emergencies and the attractions that come from being a police officer too.

51

b. **Firefighting**: Being a fire fighter is as bad as being a police officer. You are overly emotional and your emotion might ride your judgment of the situation. It will be uneasy for you to get up in a jiffy, get dressed and run off to a fire scene without thinking things twice. You would always want to do a careful thinking and proper calculation as an empath, but where is the time? Your commander is already shouting orders here and there and you would always feel you shouldn't be here. It would hurt you more if your team lost huge resources to the fire. You don't need a regular heartbreak job.

c. **Sales person**: This is the worst job an empath can pick up. Sales personnel usually have to go for long hours, stay in open places and meet a whole bunch of people. Empaths hate every one of those things, so, how do you combine your job with your nature? Your job demands that you smile at all clients as they walk in, but you are already worn out and exhausted. Your job requires direct contact with a lot of people, outspokenness and nonstop interactions. Going on with that will sap the life out of you every day. Also, you can easily pick up the emotional state of anyone among your clients.

d. **Politics**: Where do you find the energy for the stress? You are going to burn out your positive energy if you continue to go up and down in meetings, campaigns and intense political activities. You will be meeting a whole bunch of people every time, having to talk every time and picking up new energy radiation when you meet people. Something will tug at your heart every time you manage to pull yourself home. 'this isn't fun, this has to stop, shouldn't we try something different?' You would understand more if you are in the political realm already, though, I insist you heal yourself by listening to the whispers of that inner mind.

e. **Executive**: Once in a while, you would find yourself working in an executive position and it might be hard to get away, but staying on the seat would not be easy either. You would feel reluctant to impose your wishes on other people. You hate to hurt the feeling of everyone, including those who carried out poor jobs and out of pity, you will likely strike a lot of poor deals for the company. This is why it is strongly recommended that an empath should not take a very eminent position in the company, like an executive. If you hold such an office and you cannot afford to let go, hire a brilliant adviser who would not be an empath.

Now the good jobs?

These are, as I labelled them, good jobs, but you should understand that all of these won't work for you. Sometimes, you would prefer job B but not the rest. This is only a list of fields you will like thrive with your energy. So, don't find it absurd that you hate some and love the other. Find your preference and get ready to work towards it:

a. **Entrepreneurship**: You shouldn't be surprised to find this at the top. It is the joy of all empaths. In my interviews, a lot of empaths declare that they would rather work on their own than work for others. They enjoy the leisure and absence of pressure. No one would come in and scream about how slow they are or how soon they may lose their jobs. They also understand that whatever pressure they feel is what they brought by their own hands and that is fine. You cannot replace the joy of a self-controlled environment where you determine how many people you see each day. You can also shut the store and return to bed if your emotional swing is running you crazy. Your emotional swing is less likely to occur when you are yourself all the time.

b. **Arts and craft**: Arts and crafting is another field you might be exceptionally good at. It is not necessary, but you might feel the urge to paint the flowers, the crying little girl, the dying father and the cute little cat. Empaths enjoy these things a lot, and you will probably enjoy it too. If this doesn't intrigue you, try something else.

c. **Acts, Music**: Acting and Music are the next professions of empaths. Empaths love music, though not all type. You will likely subscribe to slow beat songs like American blues if you are an empath, it is the type of song released by empaths too. Most empaths prefer not to act, let's say it is because it brings them to the prying eyes of an audience, but they enjoy it for one other reason, it is their chance to take on the personality of another person. They can pretend to be someone else for a second, and they can perfectly represent what that person means.

d. **Guide, Counsellor, life coach**: You will find that you are naturally good at counselling other people if you are an empath. People look up to you for ideas, commendation, criticism and you hardly disappoint. Even the big guys walk down to listen to what you think and you always enjoy talking to them. It would seem like another person had taken over you and that person was doing all the talking, while you stood, staring in surprise. You would often return to your private corner and wonder where you got the strength and brilliance to say all that, but of course, it is in you, by default.

e. **Writers**: Becoming a writer is another profession that empaths can have no trouble taking up. As long as you are a free writer who can write on the internet or get licensed and publish as much as you like, you can write out everything you see from your heart and present them to the world. You could write about injustice, pains, life, death and every other topic that drives your spirit, as long as you find a strong means of getting people to market your skills. You may also write for organizations, firms and press teams that support your cause.

f. **Healthcare**: We both know how much you hate to see people suffer. You would always wish you could do something for them. It is the exact reason you can go into full term healthcare. Go on and help the disabled, you are not stuck in the eyes of lousy clients, instead you are among helpless and a lot of hopeless people who can live by your words of assurances. You are needed here and you would most likely thrive here. Except if you hate anything that looks like a clinic.

g. **Lawyer**: The Law is still the hope of the common man, and as someone who loves the common man, you may decide to make this your full profession. You may choose to be a lawyer so you could defend human rights, the weak, the helpless and other people who were wronged. Fair warning, you will find it extremely hard to be a prosecutor. You would always feel the passion for the person to be prosecuted and that doesn't make for a good prosecutor you know. On average, you can live a fulfilled life if you back your natural job (as a counsellor) with the job of a legal adviser.

h. **Teacher**: Teaching is a very tasking profession. It requires people who see beyond the kids they teach and the salary they get. It is a job for people who worry about the career of the children, the future of the country and the talent of each of the children. An empath would always want to give the job his best. He would always worry about possible ways to improve the children's competence. In love and tenderness, an empath would cover the psychological need of each student such that their mental growth is assisted. Perhaps, there is no better way to use your talent than this.

i. **Veterinarian**: I remember telling you that empaths are not in love with humans alone. They would often have some animals they fancy. Training and caring for an animal requires huge commitment as well. Only a person who genuinely care about them, and would not hurt them out of frustration or anger is fit for the job. That sounds like an empath. If you realize you have a special interest in animals (as a fauna empath) and your job is a dull one, you'd better sign up at the vet!

j. **Horticulturists**: Just in line with the last description, another hot cake that could suit your pastoral taste is horticulture. If you love plants originally, this may be your perfect opportunity to spend more time with your favorites. Explore more, try to understand more, appreciate them more and at the same time, increase your wealth. It is a job you won't regret s an empath.

k. **Social workers**: On a different level, you may sign up for social services too. You should consider signing up in humanitarian organizations, non-governmental organizations and so on, as this is a direct way to solve a problem of people around you, using your words, healing spirit and financial support of your organization.

Wow! That was a long list, found something you want to try out?

Chapter 8: Techniques To Improve Persuasion Skills As An Empath

Why exactly do you think empaths are reluctant to argue in public? Can you tell me the reason you think you cannot establish your position even when you were sure you were right? Convincing to see uncommon things is hard, and it is a general problem for empaths. In case you are still wondering what exactly is the source of the problem, it is persuasion skills.

Empaths are born brilliant but quiet. People who can think critically but cannot struggle. That is why you know when it is wrong, you see what no other person is seeing but you cannot push others to see what you see. You can see the loophole in the budget presented by the chairman, but no one else seems to see it and everyone is happily nodding a 'yes'. You would find it hard to stand and object because you do not want to hurt anyone's spirit. If you manage to object and every eye stares at you, you would feel a thud in your belly and you would almost blame yourself immediately.

'From the way I view this, this company might run into debts next year if such a huge amount is disbursed without a backup plan', you started. You would hardly find the words to stress what you see so that others can be convinced. And your presentation won't get any easier if the person who prepared immediately stood. "sir, you are absolutely off the point. This is a budget based on meticulous research and…." You wouldn't wait for him to finish; you are on your sit already.

In similar cases, you would argue less at home, at the gym, at school and you would make only a little effort to prove what you are trying to say to the others. Believe me, that is not the best a brilliant person like you can do, and that is why you need to hone your persuasion skills. In order to help you do that, I have drafted the next few lines and I am happy to assure you that using these skills would be a life changing experience for you. Let's go check them:

a. **Be a good listener**: Before you get people to listen to you attentively, you must have actively listened to them. Listen to them as you would listen to a classroom teacher. Not like a robot taking instructions, or a debater looking for the weak points to exploits. You are somebody trying to understand. This skill will help you to expressly understand what the speaker was trying to say, what he had not said and what could be dubious. Your brain will process and provide more helpful tips on the conversation if you get all the facts and figures straight too. This is why you must not be eager to push your ideas forward, listen first, and you will understand where, when and how to come in the talk.

b. **Laud all parties and build a common ground**: Lauding all parties is a tip that a lot of empaths hardly remember. You should remember to thank the other speakers, thank the listeners and let them know you appreciate the attention they are paying you. You should then move forward to establishing the common grounds you all have.

For example; If I would like to reject the budget proposed by the president in a board meeting. I would simply stand and begin by thanking the Chairman and his budget team for their efforts. Then move on to the patient board members who have the interest of the company at heart. Lastly, I will proceed to explain that 'though the budget looks impressive, it has some sides that our brilliant chairman and his team might have to check again.

Can you imagine the flow of that conversation in the meeting? No one would have a tough time rolling with the flow, because I have their hearts already. And without raising eyebrows, I have told them the budget isn't good enough!

c. **Don't be trivial, be businesslike from the start**: If you want to gain people's attention absolutely, don't start like a joker. Begin by going straight to the point, do not begin to talk about what came to your mind when you saw the chairman's car. Don't tell them how much you think this isn't necessary, but you decide to say it anyway. Let them understand from your tone, your agitation and your insistence that you really feel that the meeting should not be concluded without raising this issue.

You should also try not to be in a rush. Take all time you can to unravel your wonders to them step-by-step, it is a skill you must certainly have as a persuader. It is not easy; it requires a brilliant approach. This is why you can help yourself by jotting your points and arranging how you'd like to present them before you stand on your feet to give your suggestions.

d. **Appeal to their sense of emotion**; While you sit and think about the best ways to present your thoughts, don't neglect your emotion. Emotion is a powerful tool that you can use to win their hearts. The bad news is that most empaths get too emotional while presenting their case, and they often lose. Their audience realize they are getting emotional and would naturally assume they are judging the state of things by their feelings. That must not happen to you because you have read this book. You are expected to think about it carefully, know when to get emotional and when to control yourself.

For example, while I was trying to push that the budget should be reduced, I might add a picture like "ladies and gentlemen, think about the number of staffs we will lay off if this fails. Imagine how this failure can stain the reputation of each and every one of us in the papers. The media would assume we are corrupt and we were deliberately toying with the funds and lives of our investor......"

Can you imagine yourself saying that? Do you still think people would not like to listen to you? come off it, you will persuade everyone if you use the right skills at the right time.

e. **Create a picture**: It is important to create a picture in the head and heart of your listeners as you speak. Let them see what you are talking about. Let their head be filled with shuddering images of what would happen if they refuse to give you the yes you are requesting. Let them understand that everything you are trying to say is what they can agree with you on, because they can see them too.

If you construct the right words well enough, it is even possible that long after they left the sitting you had with them, they would remember the images you created in their head and they would want to listen to you more. I should not forget to tell you. Whatever image, emphasis and message you are trying to pass must be true, this is very important for you to gain your audience every time. Most empaths can see the pictures in their head, but it is never enough. Find a way to get them into the head of your audience too!

f. **Don't assume**: This isn't the first time I will remind you not to assume, it is a clear survival lesson; assumption can be fatal. Ask questions when you are not clear about something. Don't assume your wife changed because they are getting bored of you. What if there was some issue at work? That is an assumption, right. But an empath might go on to assuming not-so-exciting cases, and that is why they shouldn't even try.

g. **Show your fears and emphasize them:** I have surely mentioned something like this earlier in the conversation. But this is different from appealing to their emotions. It is about displaying your own emotions. Empaths are solution providers, you are raising that talk because you have found a problem that must be noted, whether you have the solution or not. This is why you must go all out to show that you do not only know what you are doing, you are absolutely clear about it.

It is a brilliant idea to list out the benefit of going against your suggestions, but make sure you lay much more emphasis on the danger, and find a way to make it sink in. Let's go to our old budget case. I could say to the board members: If you do not cut down this budget, we will be going all out for the investment and we will be having ripples of profits if we win, but what if we don't? Is this investment worth risking and jeopardizing the 40 years' accruement of our company?

Believe me, your opponents will meet you on the stair and tell you that you did a great job in there, even though, they'd punish you for it. Guess what? You can persuade them about that too.

h. **Nag:** Nagging isn't a nice resolution. It is an idiotic way of insisting that something is what you want. Whether idiotic or symbiotic, you have got to fall back to it if nobody is listening. You need to brace up and change from the guy who would shut down and find a sit the moment an opposition springs. Transit to the guy who would nag and nag till somebody says "okay!" or another one shouts "is that what you want? Fine!"

Wondering if nagging can ever bring that? Of course it will, as long as you keep making it a pack of brilliant declarations. That said, can you remember anyone who likes pulling you into an argument because they were sure you would give up even when you should win? Time to give them a surprise.

i. **Suggest an alternative:** Most of the time, it is not ideal to argue without having a brilliant alternative to support your claim. It is all part of the job, take all the time you need and think about a possible alternative to the problem at hand, try to see if there is some way you can solve that problem before presenting it to the other party. That is what empaths do anyway.

You have to remember however; it is not a must to find an alternative before you can voice your dissatisfaction. If you reflect on the problem and you cannot find any solution, then it isn't a bad idea to present your exact worry to the team. It is also necessary for you to bear in mind that your solution is not always the best. Sometimes, someone might have a nice idea on the problem you have pointed out. So, you should maintain a flexible ground except if that solution is what you are actually trying to pitch to them.

j. **Be confident**: Confidence is enough to win a vote-of-no-confidence. Well, it looks like that is what you are trying to win. After all, it was all set before you showed up with your ideas. Your listeners can pick up a lot from your confidence as you state your position. Other people's confidence naturally gets to us. This is exactly what you will do to them too.

Whenever you are trying to argue out a point, let your confidence be expressed as you walk up and down. Gesticulating with your hands and choosing the right words at the right moment.

You know the stunning thing? Doing all of these does not take away your nature as an empath. It does not take your inward style of life away and it is no reason you would become less emotional. Instead, it can only save you from the heartbreak of knowing that something isn't right, and dipping all hands your hands and legs to ensure that worst case doesn't happen. Now tell me, do you still think you cannot convince people on what you see about them? Cheers again.

Chapter 9: A Real Life Example

Why don't we try something different? We have spent all day talking about different things that affect an empath life. I have shown you series of ways you can get yourself out of each mess as an empath too. But I have gathered it all from my years of research, I am not an empath, and you already know how much I love empaths. As my offshore nick reads, "the empath of empaths".

But wouldn't it be more fun if we hear straight from an empath? I bet it could be eye-opening. You want to hear from a person who has lived all their life bearing that trademark that makes you odd from every other person. You want to know how others navigated their days amidst their emotional struggles and what problems they faced. Perhaps, you share the same experience and they could tell you how they resolved theirs. Isn't it? I knew that would be it and you should know I won't disappoint you.

My team set out in the country and met some empaths, we had interviews across many states. We detailed everything we heard, and trust me, you are about to read the most exciting, detailed and revealing parts of an empath's life, have fun!

An interview with Myles Richard. (A United States Art Dealing Empath from the United Kingdom)

(All seated)

Team: Hello, can we meet you ma'am?

Mrs. Richard: Yes, I am Myles Richard, an international art dealer and it feels really good to be doing this again. (all smiles)

Team: Doing what?

Mrs. Richard: Having this talk on Empathy. Many people have walked into my office, uninterested in talking about my business or La Crosse, all they want to know is what it feels like to be an empath.

Team: Does everyone know you are an empath?

Mrs. Richard: Well you can't hide a thing like that. The family had always known while I was growing. "you have a heart of gold!" dad would say, "will you drive them hard and stop acting like a little sissy!" my La Crosse coach would slam in my head, and try as I might, I remain open hearted. It isn't so hard for everyone to find out at work too.

Team: So, you are saying one can be an empath from birth?

Mrs. Richard: Absolutely! The instant you begin to grow up, everyone starts to see that you have a heart for other people. You struggle and you don't mind working yourself out just to make sure others are not hurt. You wonder why everyone can't be happy and you have a special thing for the weak, poor, hurt, and helpless. Plus, you can read minds.

Team: Can one's environment influence her empathy?

Mrs. Richard: I will say yes, though, not without exceptions. In most cases, what you see around you can influence your empathy. Your past experiences can make you love others more. How much love you get from your friends, family, people in general, those factors can tell how much you would grow to care about others unconditionally. You know, in the reverse case, even when you had no palatable experience while growing up, you might still grow to love.

Everyone hated you, you had to fend for yourself, troubles here and there, all without a friend or anyone who cares, you might still grow to love. As the saying that 'being friendless can show you exactly how to be a friend'. So you see, environment can influence your empathy a bit, but empathy is inborn, you can't help being kind to people.

Team: How was life growing up as an empath?

Mrs. Richard: Complicated!

Team: Really? How?

Mrs. Richard: Now the environment got me on this. I grew up in a great family of 4. My sister is no empath, though, she doesn't pass for a narcissist. Put her in a bit nicer class. I grew up with these people who loved me, but had no idea what empathy is about. They showed me love, but they think the amount of love I give back is very weird. Nice to everyone, never angry, never demanding, never arguing, and so forth… What an awkward child. I did well in school, and I had no issues with my colleagues. The troublesome boys broke their lockers, they fought each other in class and I cried for the wounded loser. I hated it when a teacher walked in to say someone did horribly in her tests. I often felt bad and guilty like in some way, I shouldn't have let it happen.

Team: That was from teenage, is it?

Mrs. Richard: (smiles) much earlier. At teenage, I was nice to every dick and harry and some boys thought I liked them specially. I would be off after school usually, but once in a while, I would call anyone who failed their tests and ask if I could show them after school. Many would slam me because I had little persuasion skills, but a few agreed, most of the time, they were boys. So, I sat each one as agreed and taught them. I would stare at them and read in their mind that they thought I had special thing on them. Later, they would ask me to be their girlfriend but I was forever sure I felt nothing special for them. It was always hard to say "no" to anyone though. I didn't want to hurt their feelings. I simply smiled off those talks and swerved topics to the weather and their nosy big shoes.

Team: So, you had no date, no sex at teenage?

Mrs. Richard: Right. I couldn't bring myself to do it. The girls in class were always talking about it. Now and then, a girl would walk up to me for advise on the handsome senior who'd been asking her to date him. One would be here to tell me about the guy she'd had sex with after a party last weekend. It was a thrilling experience to them, and I shared their happiness. I nursed the thought of getting into bed with someone too. But I wasn't sure there's anyone in the world I would do it with. Every time I stared at a male, I thought he was attractive, but I was sure I wouldn't do it with him because I could not feel a special connection to him, even if he had just asked me to be his girlfriend.

Team: Did you get to the university with that habit?

Mrs. Richard: Beyond. I got a job in an art store and every customer loved to queue on my stand. They trusted my opinions and they would rather talk to me or nothing. They appreciate my art and the fact that I could never bring myself to charge them exorbitantly. Men, even women asked me to be their girlfriends, but it was the same dead end. It went on till the man I married showed up.

Team: Oh, finally, you said yes to somebody!

Mrs. Richard: Come on, shouldn't I? Anyway, I didn't. We said yes to each other.

Team: Let's hear more.

Mrs. Richard: The instant I walked into the store that morning, the weather, the air, life seemed to be different. I could smell goodness in the air, but my boss would think I have gone nuts again so I kept it to myself. Then, this young man showed up. He wandered around and had no idea what to pick. He went to the secluded corners in the gallery and stood for a long while. A few staff went by him and told him what they think he should buy. But he nodded and picked none of their choices. Then, there was me behind him. "Pick that", I pointed to a pretty art of an old woman giving a bear hug to her granddaughter. He looked at me, and smiled. "Do you have a grandmother?" he asked and I told him I am at work, 'we could discuss it at dinner'. We became friends and that was how it all started. He is an empath too.

Team: Now I know exactly what I missed. You mean a male is an empath too?

Mrs. Richard: yes, it is hard to think that men would cry when they hear your stories. The society thinks little of them, and that is why most male empaths don't like to come out as one.

Team: Oh, that is fascinating. You can't be happier ever since. But just before we discuss what it is like as a couple, let's talk about your personal development. What was life like to you?

Mrs. Richard: My teachers, parents, everyone thought I was highly emotional, but it was more. I would cry when our little pet got hit by a car down street, when my sister cried because she had bad grades. "stop being so emotional" was what everyone had to say. I would fall sick the instant anyone got sick in the house, and I would come down with the same ailment. Those things got me wondering if 'being highly emotional' is the only thing I have got.

While I struggled to understand what I am and why I am so different, I would spend all of my spare time in my room, alone. I would lay in my bed and shut my eyes hard. I guess I can the atmosphere penetrating my soul and saying things to me. Don't ask me what because that might be hard to tell. I would also spend thinking about the life of other people, and wondering what should have been or what would be a better step in their lives, and that was how I spent my childhood.

It took me a long while to understand what was happening to me. I was out of high school already, and at the top of my next plan was a diploma. I became extremely curious about myself, wondering why I was the only who saw things. I was the only one who viewed things differently in the house, like I was from some strange separate planet. I researched, saw a counsellor and then I discovered the planet of empathy. I came across the concept of emotional contagion. That is the tendency to contact the emotion of another person. I discovered why other people's emotion always got to me too many times and their energy would fill my spirit.

Team: So, you grew up wondering who you are and why you are different?

Mrs. Richard: That is practically right, and you might say I spent it drawing other people's energy and solving their problems.

Team: You were always filled by other people's energy, what does that mean and how did you get over that?

Mrs. Richard: That is a big talk, and it all boils down to emotional contagion which I have explained earlier. I realized that whether I was sad or happy would not matter the minute I listened to other people's problems. I would become completely filled by their feelings. If they were happy or sad, it would get to me. I do not even have to hear you say anything before I become subsumed in your energy. If I walk by you and saw a frown on your face, I would spend all day wondering why you were unhappy, I would frown without knowing. If you are happy, I would be filled with your radiance in that same way.

The trouble with this is that people are hardly happy. There is the credit, mortgage, drunk wife, dull son and so on. Most people have a reason to be sad, and that is what they wear on their faces. By implication, that's what I pick too. I realized that this energy was not always good for me. It spoils my exuberance and it gets no better as I deal with more people who had negative energy. I began to find ways to protect my energy and make it thrive above my problems. I figured I needed strong persuasion skills too. People discard my suggestions easily, though they turned out to be right in most cases. My co-workers and my friends do not always understand what I see too. When I try to talk them into seeing what I see, they think it is all bluff and it is nothing to worry about. Those were problems I set out to resolve.

What did I do? I contacted a tantra coach who guided me through my self-discovery. I began to realize what it means to live in my own power, my own energy. My personal coach also advised me; "you should try to ground your soul every time you feel overwhelmed by other people's energy. I did those trainings and followed the instructions throughout my university days. Also, I met life coaches who advised me on persuasions skills. sometimes, "learn to nag till they give you a yes", be a good listener and try to provide an alternative to what you see. I read a whole lot of good books too.

By the end of the lessons, I knew I was a different empath. I became changed and I was less absolved in other people's energy. I could listen more and offer suggestions and people would not think it is a bluff. It is why people are thrilled to hear my suggestions and they are thrilled to use them at my art store.

Team: How do you advice empaths to find themselves so they can live a thrilling life?

Mrs. Richard: If you are an empath and you are having trouble finding yourself. My first advice is that you should take all the time you need to find yourself. Be patient. Then take tantra lessons, it will really help you discover yourself. Learn to ground yourself and build a team of people who can life your spirit. There are some people who certainly care. Talk to them. Let them understand how much you need them to keep you vibrant and alive. Stay away from negative people too, and make sure you spend some time to sort yourself out, alone.

Team: How about your love life?

Mrs. Richard: My love life is the most amazing part of the whole story. My husband knows am I an empath, and I had no trouble getting to know he is one too. We found it easy to talk to each other, and sometimes, to stay away from each other. We have heard stories of empaths who didn't live in a bedroom with their partner, but that wasn't our story, we were together when we could be. My husband often think about my problems, work out solutions for me while I spent my time thinking about his own problems. So, I am always amused when he walks into the room to tell me that he had finally found the solution to what I should be worried about. In his own case too, it thrills him. We were always thinking about other people, and finally, we are in the thoughts of someone at least.

A lot of other people still approach us for advise, and my husband doesn't mind if I have a private chat with a man. He can swear on his life that I won't cheat, I can too. So, it wasn't so hard in marriage.

Team: What is your final word on empathy?

Mrs. Richard: You are very lucky to be an empath. You and I can help people live a happy life. We can solve problems and we can make our voices known without compromising our nature. Find your voice, discover yourself and follow advice from experts. Life is an experience you will enjoy.

Conclusion.

Phew! That was a long talk! But that was good too. If you, or your child is an empath and you have just read every word of this, I bet you have just discovered a whole lot of different things about yourself. You now understand who you are, and what life could seem while you are still growing.

You know what you should and shouldn't have done in different cases. You can imagine what life was like as an empath in the old days and today, you can tell what kind of empath you are. You know the various ways you can solve your problems and how best you can help your energy thrive. I am sure I told you what life can be like in sex, relationships and work. I certainly told what to expect at work too. There was a long list of different styles you can employ to persuade even your opponents.

Anything else? I am really confident you have anything you need to enjoy life as a brilliant empath that you are. If you think there is one other thing you need, trust me, it is hidden in those pages, go through them again. If you still think there is something else though, I will be glad to attend to you. I hope I am able to help you, bye, and remember to drop some great comments, thanks!